Carol

The Story of my Life

Refugees writing in Oxford

Filda Lukonyomoi Otunnu

HASAN BAMYANI

THE STORY OF MY LIFE

Refugees writing in Oxford

Edited by CAROLE ANGIER

Photographs by Asylum Welcome
photography projects, 2003–5

THE CHARLBURY PRESS

OXFORDSHIRE

ISBN 0 9546342 4 1

A catalogue record for this book is available from the British Library

This edition first published by the Charlbury Press, June 2005

Printed in the United Kingdom by the Alden Press, Oxford. This publication is printed on acid-free paper

The Charlbury Press is an imprint of Day Books,
www.day-books.com

Contents

Acknowledgements

The Story of My Life was produced with the assistance of Asylum Welcome, whose Education Committee also organised the writing classes.

Carole Angier's fee was paid by the Royal Literary Fund.

We sincerely thank both the RLF and Asylum Welcome for their support.

We thank especially Mercedes Cumberbatch, Director of Asylum Welcome, and Sister Bernadette, Jean Kaye and Terence Ranger of the Education Committee; and also Clive Gillham, who gave us a big, light room in St Francis House for our meetings.

The quotation from Günter Grass (*Rede vom Verlust*, Steidl Verlag, Göttingen; English translation, *The Future of the German Democracy*, Crossroad/Continuum, New York) is reproduced by kind permission of the publishers. The quotation from Dan Pagis is reproduced by kind permission of the translators Anthony Rudolf and Miriam Neiger-Fleischmann; grateful acknowledgement is made to the estate of Dan Pagis. The excerpt from 'Song of an Émigré', from *Without End* by Adam Zagajewski (translated by Clare Cavanagh, Renata Gorczynski, Benjamin Ivry and C.K. Williams; copyright © 2002 by Farrar, Straus and Giroux, LLC) is reprinted by permission of Farrar, Straus and Giroux, LLC.

We also thank Rory Carnegie, Nikki van de Gaag and the photographers of the *Our Journeys, Our Clothes Our City* and *Picturing Oxford* projects for their splendid photographs.

Last but not least, we thank our publisher, Edward Fenton of Day Books, for his generosity and hard work.

Author biographies

Ali Askari came from Afghanistan over three years ago as an unaccompanied minor. He has attended courses in English and IT and has completed the International Study Programme at Oxford College. He has now been offered places at Sussex University and at Oxford Brookes to read Law, but is unable to take up a full-time degree course, as he is still on TA (Temporary Admission).

He is currently continuing his education with A-levels and is very active in the Afghan community in Oxford. He also does voluntary work with the Youth Worker at Asylum Welcome.

Hassan Bamyani was a teacher in Afghanistan. When he fled three and a half years ago he was forced to leave his wife and children behind in Iran. Unless his ELR (Exceptional Leave to Remain) is changed to ILR (Indefinite Leave), he cannot bring his family here to join him.

He completed two years of journalism at university before leaving Kabul. Since arriving in the UK, he has attended courses in English, including Academic English, and IT. He now has a place on 'Pathways to IT', an Access course for entry to university.

Hassan has written a book of poetry in Farsi which he hopes will be translated.

Eden Habtemichael was a journalist in Eritrea. She came here four years ago and has been given ILR.

As well as bringing up her daughter,

Segen, she has attended classes in English and IT and has now applied for a degree course in Information Systems and Multi-Media. She hopes to be a writer again in Britain.

Segen is six years old. She goes to school in Oxford.

Mohammed Issa's family fled from Chad to Sudan when he was a boy, and he arrived here from Sudan five years ago. He has worked full time ever since.

Wakunyeki Mukobya came from Congo five years ago and was given ELR. She was a qualified nurse in her own country but needed to learn English before she could think of retraining. In order to keep her skills up-to-date, she has done voluntary work at the Churchill Hospital and trained with the St John's Ambulance. She has progressed to courses in Drug Calculation and English with Medical Application. She is trying to get her ELR converted to ILR in order to resume her nursing career.

Filda Lukonyomoi Otunnu came from Uganda in 1989. She brought seven dependants with her, but lost her husband and son. She herself narrowly escaped with her life after a brutal beating which has left her semi-disabled.

Since graduating from the University of Derby in 2003, Filda has worked as a volunteer for Asylum Welcome and for the Oxford Development Education Centre. She is also a founder and co-ordinator of BK.LUWO, a Ugandan community women's group, which works against isolation and for the preservation of heritage.

'Refuge in Amuru' is part of a book she hopes to publish, and we are grateful for her permission to include it here.

'Window': photograph by Behar

Introduction

My first biographical subject, Jean Rhys, used to say that when she wrote something down it went away. And my second, Primo Levi, wrote about his experiences of Auschwitz as soon as he returned, in order to relieve his burden of memories, and to tell the world.

When I proposed a creative writing class for refugees and asylum seekers in Oxford, I hoped it might help them to do the same: to exorcise their memories, and to tell them to the rest of us. You are reading this book, so my second hope may actually be realised. But about the first I am not so sure.

Some of our meetings were shot through with pain. In one, Ali could not finish his poem about his mother – though he did return to it later. When Eden wrote about her first months in this country, alone with her baby daughter, facing a hostile and uncertain future, the recollection overwhelmed her. And when I read back to Filda her account of what happened to her and her daughters at Amuru, her eyes filled with tears. In those moments, expressing their memories made them 'come back and seize you like a spider,' as Hassan said; which is why people often stay silent.

On the other hand, through her tears Filda kept nodding firmly and saying 'Yes. Yes, that's true.' She wanted to tell her story, just as Primo Levi had done. And she wanted to tell it clearly and compellingly, so that everyone would listen. She wouldn't get rid of her pain. But she could turn it into something else as well: knowledge and art, an object of value to other people.

Filda felt this first because she has been here longest; the others are much newer arrivals. But as the classes gathered pace the same desire gripped them all: not just to tell their stories, but to tell them well; to make something durable of their loss and pain. In other words, they became not just tellers of their stories but writers, looking not just for words, but for the best words. And our meetings became mostly joy.

When Omid realised that 'accidentally' did not mean 'all at once' and the word he wanted was 'suddenly', he punched the air like a footballer after a goal. Eden wanted to use a vital organ as an image of importance, and found 'blood vessel' in her dictionary; when I suggested 'heart' instead, she clasped her hand over her own heart in pleasure. When Filda and I found the words 'toppling' and 'slurred' for her story about her father, she was as excited as a little girl. And Hassan's journey of discovery through English was an adventure every week. One day he asked, 'What is new flower called?' 'Bud,' I said. He liked the word so much he wrote a line then and there: 'The bud with its baby mouth cried *Wah wah...* .'

This passionate pursuit of words was necessary because English was no one's native language, and was still quite new to everyone but Filda, who has been in Britain for seventeen years. Wakunyeki, after only five, translated her poetry from French with very little help from me. But all the others needed English advice; and everyone wanted writing advice, which is what I was there for.

So the poems and stories that follow have been edited by me. I suggested cuts, expansions and re-orderings; and I corrected grammar, and offered better words. Sometimes the original words or grammar were so fractured that I couldn't understand what the writers meant, and had to ask them to explain – whereupon what they said was often so good that we put it in. That is how Hassan's poem *The Rug Speaks* got its lines 'Why do you give me/only your feet?', and how Eden's *Sweet Lily* got the lines 'When I heard music/She danced/When I was angry/She stayed still.' But the ideas were always the writers' own. All I did was interpret and edit.

I have worked with quite a few writers over the years, but this class was different. Partly because I saw not just a new language open out to them, but a whole new world. And partly because of what Ali says in the poem on the back cover: that these stories are true.

That made this work, for me, a uniquely moving experience. And also for them. It changed his life, Mohammed said; it made him see that communication with English people was possible, and he has since designed a website for Chadians in Britain. I hope it will be a moving experience for you, the reader, as well. I think it will.

CAROLE ANGIER
BIOGRAPHER AND CLASS TEACHER

'Oxford light': photograph by Behar

There

Loss has given me a voice. Only what is entirely lost demands to be endlessly renamed: there is a mania to call the lost thing until it returns. Without loss there would be no literature.

GÜNTER GRASS, '*On Loss*'

'Hands': photograph by Daphne

My Grandparents

They were kind to me,
Very kind – you can't imagine –
My grandfather, who died at 45,
Before I was even born,
My grandmother, who died at 93

Now their house is a museum.
They are my heritage, and my barrier
Against Africa's war

Through these high, dust-free halls,
Where Africa's temperature and humidity are regulated,
I walk at ease

I never tire of these treasures,
Their variety does not exhaust me.
Each object is a witness to its own survival.
Work endures beyond its time.
Such proof supports me

Yet no one remembers who they were,
My grandparents,
Obscure existences of which I am
The final product,
The memorial

England,
I am their museum.
I merit exhibition here.

WAKUNYEKI MUKOBYA

My Grandmother

She stood so tall and graceful.
Her skin was much lighter than mine.
She walked gingerly and gracefully,
Like the tils I used to see on my savannah farm.

I don't remember her laughing,
But how she rolled those light green pobo leaves.
The next thing I noticed was –
Thick grey smoke from her mouth!

Was it the smoke that coloured her teeth?
They were not as white as mine,
But they seemed stronger and healthier.
None was wobbly, like mine.

Why did she smoke?
Was it because she was strong, like a man?
Her husband respected her.
He followed her instructions and obeyed her commands.

Other women came to her.
In the sowing season
She mixed their seeds
and scattered them in the fields.

It was her instruction
That from the first cow milk be given
To the treasured fifth child.
He, Uncle John,

Squatted with a rope, held wisely,
And with the other hand
Bound both hind legs of the victim.
Hands flew, hooves kicked

Only the kabu stayed still,
Jammed between his knees.
The hands grabbed the udder
and suddenly a bright white stream
hit the jar.

When she knew her time had come
And many people would celebrate her passing
She asked for a bull's liver for her last meal
And her husband picked
The choicest bull

The aroma of frying liver stroked her nose,
She closed her eyes as if in sleep.
So tall and graceful,
Her skin lighter than mine,
She was dead.

FILDA OTUNNU

My Mother

Sounds and echoes
Everybody is happy,
   Excited

   No fears.
   Yes, no
   Fears. All you can see is love
   Flying everywhere
   With the peace dove

Later

   The sounds and echoes change their
   Rhythm
   Not laughing but crying
      What happened?
   No it cannot be happening
   Sounds of rockets
      On our beautiful village

A seven-year-old boy is playing
The sounds annoy him
Still he sits on the ground without knowing

What?

   Hand reaching for me
   Towards my shoulder
   Pulling and
   Saving
   My life

Who?

Is there sacrifice?
   Yes
   The hand is falling
   I can't see I don't know who
   The hand!!!
   The body vanishing in smoke
   Never seen again

That saving ray lit up
Once
To give the boy a chance
Of life
Of dance

Who?

   The one who loves?
   Yes
   Mother and her hand
   Made my life and saved it
   And now I am alone
   With her story in my heart's beat

Mother!

   You gave your spirit
   To your future generations

   Thanks, thanks
   I will tell your heroic story
   I will pass on your tragic history

   To all
   The world

ALI ASKARI

My Father

A young man full of passion and energy to serve the nation, to help the nation, to die for the nation.

He is a soldier for the Ministry of Defence. He can see the deprivation of the people and wants to help them. He wants to show them what he feels is the best way – freedom, and the right to say what they think.

The Revolution of the Mujahedin starts, the government is collapsing, everywhere is war and dying. He decides to leave the capital and to help his own tribe, a nation deprived of their rights for nearly 250 years. Yes! He is going home, to the city where he was born, where the people are dying of famine, and where they have no education to make their own future.

He founds a small party, a political and military party to represent these people in a future government. He wants to help the lowest class of society, the disadvantaged. He wants to give them hope, to tell them that a cruel and tyrannical government deprived them of their rights.

Now he is a commander, a commander full of sympathy and understanding. Thousands of people follow his order and command.

He established hundreds of centres for the Hazarah people, where their rights could be discussed, and their role in a future Afghan government. But it did not last long. From the dirty hands of the Taliban came Hazarajat, and took this great soul from his people.

I am proud of you, Father!

I and all Hazarah generations to come will follow you. We will serve our nation as you did. And you will be the hero and martyr for me and for all.

This is a very very short story of my father's life.

ALI ASKARI

My Mother

Once upon a time, a long long time ago, I was asleep in the morning when I heard my brother's voice. He was crying. I woke, and sat up and called him.

'Hussain, why are you crying?'

'Hassan,' my brother replied. 'Hassan, our mother has died.'

I started to cry with him. My brother took me to the mosque where my mother's body was lying. When we arrived it was very crowded. The people gave way before us. In the room they uncovered my mother's face.

When I saw my mother, she looked as though she was asleep. I started to shout and cry. After a few minutes they took me out. Since then I have not seen my mother's face.

HASSAN BAMYANI

My Mother

My father was away and my mother was out in the fields.

I remember my cousin, who is about two years older than me, came to our house. She was living with our grandparents, whose house was just a few metres away, on the other side of the road that runs along our land.

My cousin told me she could make some kwon, which is our bread. She suggested that we compete. I was only about three years old.

So we built the fire in my mother's kitchen and I made my first kwon. My cousin brought hers over for tasting. Hers tasted different from the usual kwon that I was used to, and she said she had added some sugar. Mine was simple. I made it as my mother did: by boiling water, adding the millet flour, and kneading it with a wooden spoon until the dough was ready, then leaving it in the fire until it was brown.

My mother returned from the fields and I offered her my first meal. While she was tasting it I sat on her lap and suckled some milk from her breast.

I was afraid she would not like it because it was not sweet, like my cousin's. But then she said my kwon was very good and well done, and I was proud.

Filda Otunnu

26

My Father

I remember he once danced with me. He held both my hands in both his hands, and we slid our feet from side to side.

With each movement, from side to side, he sang a tune:'*Sure sure sure my boy.*' Never did I hear any *Sure sure my girl.* I questioned that in my heart, but I didn't ask why.

Usually he was not at home. But when he was, he sat with other men. My mother served him and waited on him. Every night she polished his wooden sandals and brought them to him. Everyone looked up to him. To me there was no man superior to him, and when he was there I felt safe.

Then one night voices woke me from my sleep. Without fear, I entered our living room. The hurricane lamp was burning low, but I could see my father and a couple of other men. My stepmother had served them their dinner. In front of them the bottle of arege was almost empty.

On the table there were toppling heaps of coins. My father was struggling to count them, but each pile kept tunbling down like a waterfall. And as he counted his words were slurred, as though they were falling down too. Again I questioned that in my heart, but didn't ask why.

One evening, it happened. We were sitting outdoors, and the moon and stars were shining brightly. Suddenly there was the sound of a bicycle bell, and my father arrived. My mother and stepmother wanted to get up, but I remembered the table manners he had taught me: do not get up from the table until your plate is empty. I reminded them, and they obeyed. My father stopped and looked at us. And all of a sudden he dropped his bicycle, and ran towards us, and began hitting my mother and stepmother furiously.

I watched his hands moving, from side to side, from side to side, and I knew I would never feel safe again.

FILDA OTUNNU

Golden Words

The day after, spirits woke me from my bed.
Full of tears I sat on my chair.
    That day, that day …
Black spot in my life.
It has happened.

When I see his eyes in the photo frame
The bright memories come back
    But he is gone …
Still I try to speak to him
And suddenly he's there

'Are you all right, my dear?'
'Yes, father.'
'Do you remember the words I spoke to you?
 Where will you keep them?'
'Maybe in the secret diary you signed for me.'
'But why will you hide them away?'
'They are not hidden, father, but deep inside me,
Always fresh, like the air at home.'

I open the golden folder
Of my father's golden words.
'Always look far and all around,
Like a deer.
In every weather
Try everything
Learn and work and fight
Be happy, and even when you're not,
Smile.'

Dear father,
You are not only my father,
You are my brother, my guide, my friend.
    I thank you
In every weather, every day.
I will never forget your golden words.

EDEN HABTEMICHAEL

My Parents

They loved me too much – but
they were torn from me by war.
Do not cry, do not weep, my mourning
cannot bring them back
to this unjust world

What must I do, what can I say?
You cannot
believe the unbelievable

Unbelievable but true
They died on the same day –
Horrible
I refuse to remember

Who told me my place in the world?
Who took centuries to produce me
to give me life
to teach me
to encourage me?

Only language releases me
which has no dimensions
which demands no local habitation
which sets me free

But they could not survive
in this unjust world
Oh God look after
their spirits

WAKUNYEKI MUKOBYA

Sediga

Once upon a time an angel was living in a city which was set on fire. Now, angels have the finest wings and the most delicate bodies; they live in Paradise, and play with flowers, and wear only silken garments, because any other material would hurt their sensitive skin.

But this angel's paradise was set on fire. Her silken clothes caught fire, her sun-like face was darkened by dust and smoke. The angel, who was called Sediga, was like the sun engulfed by a thick, dark cloud.

She tried to live in the dark and the dust. She wanted to scream, but the bravery God had given her kept her silent. She was young, but the monster of war had taken her mother. The fire of war, the rain of bullets and missiles, and worst of all the destruction of her hopes pressed in on her. Sediga, the angel without food, without clothes, without a mother, was trapped like a fly in the web of a spider.

In reality, Sediga was one of my students. She was the best of my students; but every day and every month I saw her in the same dress, which she washed and wore again. For all those days and months she had only one dress, and one pair of shoes, which had lost their heels and most of their uppers, and were in truth only half a pair of shoes. And she never had enough to eat. But she never let this show; she never let anything show but beauty and bravery.

At last I couldn't bear it any more. My daughter was the same age and height as Sediga; so one day she and I took some of her clothes to school, to give them to Sediga. But how were we to do it? This girl who was so proud and fine, as straight as steel, how could I give her charity? I lost courage. I went to another of my best students, Hamida. 'Dear Hamida,' I said, 'we have brought these clothes for Sediga, but we daren't give them to her. Can you help us?'

Hamida and I had talked as quietly as we could, but Sediga was not fooled. Her mind is as delicate as her angel's body, and she

31

knew immediately what we were talking about. She threw us an angry look and walked away. She had never been ashamed before, but now we had shamed her.

So the sad situation continued, Sediga went on coming to school in her single dress and her half-shoes.

It was in Kabul City we were living: in the heart of my land, which was being reduced to ashes by madness and stupidity. And we were living in the south of the city, the part most devastated and destroyed by war. But I refused to give up my job as a teacher. I could not sit at home and do nothing. Even though the windows and doors of my school had been stolen, the building still stood. I went on going to school every day at 8, and coming home at 1. And despite everything I was happy, helping the poor children to learn to read and write, and giving them hope for the future.

But our people and our country were burning up in violent warfare, their lives were hell and their future dark, and I was suffering for them. And because I was equally a part of our country, I was suffering for myself as well. I was growing weaker; my body and mind were giving way, and the children were losing their teacher.

At last the day came when I could not go to school. I couldn't leave my bed; I couldn't teach my students; I lost consciousness altogether.

One of my students, Mohammed Ali, lived nearby. My wife said to my daughter, 'Hagar, tell Mohammed Ali to go and tell your father's students that he cannot come to school today.' He was not to tell them the true reason, and they were not to come and see me, because it was too dangerous to travel in that terrible time, and we didn't want anything to happen to them.

Mohammed Ali went to school, but he could not tell a lie, and he told the children what had happened to me.

I was lying on my bed, and in my half-conscious daze I heard Sediga's voice, and my wife's voice, and my wife was saying: 'Your teacher is ill and unconscious; we must not wake him up, or he will become worse still.'

But Sediga's voice woke me, and I screamed her name – 'Sediga!' So they knew I knew she was there, and they came in, Sediga and all my students, and my fellow teachers as well. I wanted to stand up to show my respect for them, and to show them that nothing terrible had happened, that they needn't worry about me, and make their troubles worse by adding another. I had taught them that I was leading them towards a bright future, and the last thing I could bear was to destroy their hopes myself.

So I rose and walked towards them, to ask how they were, and to kiss their heads and faces. But then the worst thing happened, worse than if I had never got up at all. I fell down in front of them, and could not stand up again.

I felt hands lift me up and put me on my mattress and lay me down to sleep again. But I couldn't sleep. I saw my students, young birds trapped in the fire of war, and all I could think of was the need to teach, which filled my mind.

I managed to sit up. I asked for a book, which one of them gave me. I stood up on my mattress and told them to take up their books as well: now I thought that I was not at home any more, but back in my classroom. They started to cry, saying 'Teacher, please sit down, you are not well and cannot teach.'

But slowly, as I recognised them, my children, the other teachers, I began to feel better. I understood that I was at home, not at school; God helped me to understand that I was ill, and they had come to ask me how I was.

I sat down and talked to them. But I felt ashamed that I could not teach, that I could not help them. If I could not help, I was a traitor to my people and to history, and my conscience tormented me.

My wife prepared food and drink, and we ate together, until they left us at 3 in the afternoon. As they left I saw Sediga pick up my shoes and kiss them. Thus she tried to show her love for me, and her desire not to leave me, who was her father, her teacher and her hope.

When I saw what Sediga had done I was plunged into the

33

deepest despair. I could think only of the poor children, the innocent children, in this disaster without solution, which had taken even their teacher away.

HASSAN BAMYANI

Lyla and Majnon*

Once upon a time, a long long time ago, there lived two lovers, Lyla and Majnon.

When they were children, Lyla and Majnon did not know each other, because they lived far apart, Lyla in a village and Majnon in the capital city.

When Lyla was still small her mother died, and she became an orphan. Her father remarried, but her step-mother did not care for her. Lyla went to live with her aunt, and her aunt kept her as her daughter.

One day Lyla's aunt decided to leave the village and come to the capital city. Here Lyla grew taller and more beautiful every day. But her aunt was very poor and their lives were hard. When a friend asked if Lyla could come and live with her, her aunt agreed.

But this woman was a widow and a poor woman too, and she could not keep Lyla any better than her aunt. So, although Lyla was only nine years old, she sent her out to work, cleaning the houses and looking after the children of rich people. Lyla worked very hard, and suffered very much, but still she grew more and more beautiful.

At last, when Lyla was twelve, the woman decided that she should stop working, and go to live with the woman's sister. This was the most fortunate decision, because the sister's family were good religious people, and because in this way the meeting of Lyla and Majnon came nearer.

Majnon's mother had also died when he was a child, but his father did not remarry, and his elder sister took care of the children. Majnon was a good boy and a brilliant pupil, and both his father and his teacher loved and supported him.

But then things began to change. Majnon's sister married and left the family, and his brothers left as well. Worst of all was the

*Lyla and Majnon are classic lovers in Persian literature. This is, nonetheless, Hassan's own story.

situation in his country, with war and occupation, and thousands of people killed and wounded. And now Majnon's father was old and could not work any longer. Finally he had no choice. He went to live with relatives, and sent Majnon to live with another family.

So Majnon started a new and difficult life. He and his new family were poor, but they were kind and honest, and the ideal family for him. So Majnon grew up happy and full of pride, and when he was seventeen he began studying at college.

Now, this was the fortunate thing which I have told you: because it was to Majnon's new family that Lyla came.

The very first time Majnon saw Lyla he was instantly attracted to her. He was so attracted that he nearly made a terrible mistake. Thinking she was one of the sisters in his new family, he went over and touched her head. Lyla was shocked, and asked who this rude and wicked boy was. But one of their new sisters explained that Majnon was a good boy, and it was only a mistake.

After that Lyla and Majnon became very close, like sister and brother. Majnon called Lyla his sister, and every day they understood each other more. Every day their faith grew too, and every day Lyla seemed more beautiful to Majnon.

Lyla was not only beautiful but good. She was kind to Majnon's father, who found it hard to walk; and whenever he came to see Majnon, Lyla would give him her arm and help him to walk.

Majnon's father thus came to love Lyla, and one day he asked Majnon if he would like him to ask their new mother if she would give Lyla to Majnon as his wife. Now Majnon had dreamed of this for a long time, but his religion forbade him from asking for Lyla's hand himself. Now he was afraid that Lyla would think this was a trick, and that it was he who had made his father ask if she would be his wife.

For a long time Lyla and Majnon had slept beside each other as sister and brother. All this time Majnon's love for Lyla had burned inside him, but he had never shown her his love, because he did not want to alarm her, or to lose their precious friendship.

For Majnon's best hope was Lyla's happiness. Her lovely round white face became his moon, her heavy golden hair became his sun, and with her sweet and good ways Lyla became his angel.

Majnon felt he could not live without Lyla, but that even when she was not there her spirit was inside him. She was necessary to his life, like salt to his food, like medicine when he was ill; like the light of the moon in a dark night, like a breath of warmth in the winter.

Just to look at Lyla kept Majnon alive. But he could not show her his love, because they were sister and brother, and called the same woman mother; and he wanted her to feel happy and safe.

But Allah was merciful to Majnon, and from the beginning of time He had decreed that Lyla and Majnon would be as one.

One day Majnon's father asked their mother for Lyla's hand for his son. Majnon was angry and ashamed, and he left the house and went away, saying to his mother that if she spoke to Lyla he would never come home. But he could not live without seeing Lyla's face, and after only a week he returned. His heart fluttered like a bird, thinking that perhaps his mother had spoken. But she had not spoken.

HASSAN BAMYANI

Fire I

A woman dug her field
The rain beat the ground
The rootless grass covered the ground
The sun beat the rootless grass on the ground

The woman torched the rootless grass
The fire licked the rootless grass
The wind blew
The fire roared

The flame devoured the air
It devoured the rootless grass
It rushed to the edge of the field
Where the neighbours' houses were

The woman snatched a branch of a tree
She beat the greedy fire
The flame soared high
The angry fire roared over her

She fought the fire ruthlessly
Though her anger turned to fear
She dashed through the flame this way and that
Still she beat the fire until she won

But the fire did not die quietly
It taught the woman a great lesson:
Never start a fire alone
Or you will fight it alone

And over you will always soar
The terrible memory
Of fire

FILDA OTUNNU

Fire II

Year after year
Bush fires clear the park
Crossing rivers and fields
Leaving behind the small corpses of animals and birds

Nests are tossed high
Eagles have fire on their wings
Sometimes they fall on grass roofs
And bring the fires home

First the horizon is red
Then the flames are in the valley
And we see nothing, only hear
A distant roar

It is time to torch our fields
And meet the fire half-way
Evening-time is best, when
It s not too windy

But this morning the wind
Changed. It cut me off on the safer side.
With my baby on my back
We are going to be eaten alive

Then that brave man Okello ran under the fire.
He scooped the baby from my back and yelled
To me to follow him. Bending,
Folding the baby inside his chest,

He ran under the fire to safety.
And I bent over too, and ran.
We were safe.
My baby was too shocked to cry.

FILDA OTUNNU

School

Children always have many memories from their school days. School memories are unforgettable because they are the first memories.

Now I am going to write about my first school memory. In my country children do one year pre-school. This class is like kindergarten, but it is held in the main school building to accustom children to the school environment.

When I was six years old, I had to start pre-school. I went happily. I was so glad that finally I was grown up and I could go to school like other children. On the first day, I became friends with a boy who looked a bit older than me, in the play ground before going in to class.

When it was time to go in to the classroom I followed him, because I didn't know where to go. Therefore I went to his classroom and sat down next to him.

The teacher came in. She said hello and introduced herself. She asked everyone to say their names as she checked the register. I was afraid because when I saw the others, they were relaxed, but I felt that something was wrong with me. When she asked my name, I said it very quietly, and she couldn't hear. I tried again; she checked her register book. My name wasn't on it. She said, 'Something may be wrong.' She asked me, 'How old are you?' I said 'Six,' and she said 'Ohhhh! These children are eight years old. You are in the wrong classroom.'

I felt I had made the biggest mistake of my life. But she smiled and very kindly said, 'It doesn't matter. You can stay with us, and I will take you to your classroom.'

OMID KORDANY

My Home Country

My home country is Eritrea, which is in the north-east of Africa, on the border of the Red Sea.

The population of Eritrea is three million. In this small country there are nine ethnic groups in six zones and cities. Each group has its own tradition, culture, dress, religion and language. These are Saho, Tigre, Kunama, Afar, Hidarib, Blen, Rashaida, Arabic and Tigrigna. Tigrigna is the dominant language, spoken by 70% of the population.

The weather is inviting. There are nine months of sunshine every year, and three months of rain, though even then it is not cold. The temperature varies from 20 to 30 degrees Centigrade. Chains of mountains, ancient sites, important arts and crafts and bold modern buildings are all very attractive. The Italians called the capital city, Asmara, 'the second Rome'.

The main economic resource of Eritrea is agriculture. Cereal crops, cotton and coffee are the most important products. Most of the producers are subsistence farmers. However, all the food brought to the markets is fresh and organic.

Because of colonisation the infrastructure of our educational system is very poor. There are a few private schools and colleges; and in the state system one university, fifty secondary and fewer than one hundred junior and elementary schools, one polytechnic and one nursing college.

Our government is military, with a President and Parliament.

Eritrea was colonised for centuries, first by Turkey, then by Italy, and after that by Britain and Ethiopia. In 1961 Ethiopia broke the law which protected the UN-created federation of Ethiopia and Eritrea, and recolonised my country for thirty years. After thirty years of war, in 1990 we finally gained our independence. But ten years later war broke out between Ethiopia and Eritrea once again.

Finally, I would like to say that even though there is still a war in our country, the people of Eritrea are as kind and friendly as ever.

EDEN HABTEMICHAEL

Traditional Festival in Eritrea

In Eritrea we celebrate many holidays. The traditional holiday festivals of the year are: one in September, called 'Kudus Yohanes', Saint John; a New Year and Christmas day in January called 'Lidet'; Epiphany Day, called 'Timket'; and in April Easter, called 'Fasika'. All the names of the holidays have their own meanings. All the holiday festivals are celebrated with different traditional costumes, food and music.

Let's concentrate on the festival of Saint John. This festival peaks on the 1st of September, which is the beginning of the new year in the Eritrean calendar, the 'Geaz calendar'. Celebrations start at the end of August. During the five special days called 'Pagumen', early in the morning all the girls and women between fifteen and forty-five go to the river to wash their bodies in cold water, and sing a song:

This cold water is for our health
Come, everybody, join us ….

The young unmarried girls bang on a traditional drum and sing a song to beg money for the celebrations, and the boys cut twigs from the bushes and bind them together to make burning torches called 'Hoyo-Hoyo'. In the evening before the 1st of September the girls, wearing traditional costumes and hairdos, sing a song and dance. The boys, holding up their burning Hoyo-Hoyos, knock on everyone's door, and they too sing a song until people give them money. Finally, boys and girls play ritual games the whole night in the fields. The boys may choose their future wives, and if the girl agrees the couple become engaged in the next few days.

In the morning everybody dresses in white and the children must wear new clothes.

After church a sheep is slaughtered. The people cook the meat in four or five different dishes; women make a traditional drink called 'Siwa', and traditional coffee.

At the end all the families celebrate together with their neighbours and friends in the house of the oldest person. They exchange gifts, and there is eating and dancing all day. It is a happy family day, and they make a wish for the coming year.

EDEN HABTEMICHAEL

Leaving Home

Here in this transport
I am Eve
With Abel my son
If you see my older son
Cain son of Adam
Tell him that I

DAN PAGIS,
'Written with a Pencil in a Sealed Wagon'

'Freeland': photograph by Behar

Refuge at Amuru

At first the UPDA commander threatened to burn me and my children alive in our house. But instead he ordered his troops to escort us to the Village of Faith, where they entered all the houses and looted whatever they could.

We stayed there a day and a night, but I was in great pain. The next morning I went to the Amuru Catholic Mission and asked for their help. The parish priests, Father Chris Ocan and Father Peter Olum, agreed. They registered my family as refugees, examined me and gave me medication.

One day, when I felt much better, I went to give instructions about our domestic animals. In my absence my older daughter Petua and two of her cousins decided to go back to the Village of Faith to fetch bananas and sugar cane. They had only gone a short distance when they were arrested by some armed soldiers. My bold daughter asked why they were being detained. One of the soldiers said, 'I know who you are.' It was because they knew she was Lukonyomoi's daughter. Nonetheless, after a time they allowed the children to return to the Mission, with strict instructions not to be caught outside it again.

I worried about many things – where would we be at the beginning of the school term? How would I pay the children's fees? But all my previous worries faded when it became clear that our presence was not welcome any more. The parish Mother Superior asked me to move to a desolate bungalow at the back of the parish. Its walls were partly destroyed and its rooms wet and soiled with human urine; the whole area stank, and was woefully unhealthy.

How could I take my children to such a place? And my four-year-old suffered from asthma, and my six-year-old from bone pain. ... Now I knew the agony of beggars and homeless people. I looked back over my life to see how I had dealt with those who had fled their homes and taken refuge with us, and I was grateful to remember that we had always made them welcome.

When Father Peter Olum heard what the Mother Superior had

done he told me not to listen to anyone in the Mission except the two who had accepted us, and he ordered that we should stay where we were. But the Devil does not rest. When Father Chris Olan returned from a visit to Gulu he told me that the Bishop was afraid our presence was a danger to the parish. The NRA government and the UPDA fighters both knew that we were there, and were planning to destroy the Mission if it continued to shelter us. 'Mrs Lukonyomoi must do something to save the Mission,' the Bishop had said. 'You mean we must leave?' I asked. 'Yes,' said Father Chris. I could not believe the news, and started to cry.

That night was one of the worst nights of my life. The children looked to me for wisdom and support. I cried so much that my headache returned, and that night and the next day were filled with pain. But I told my sister-in-law and the children that I would take them to my parents in Lango district, and that God would protect us on the road.

Father Peter came to me. He told me not to take to heart what the Bishop had said, and he instructed Sister Stellar to give me Phenobarbitone for my pain. He said we must not leave the Mission because if we did so we might well be killed, and our blood would be on their heads.

What was I to do? Whom was I to obey, the Bishop and the senior parish priest, or the junior priest with the sympathetic heart? I saw that our presence was sowing discord among them, and I decided to put my trust in God. I asked Father Peter to allow my sister-in-law to remain with my two youngest children, who could not walk the long distance to my parents' home, 120 miles away. I was sure that God would find a way to unite us again, for it is written: *'The Lord will also be a refuge for the oppressed, a refuge in times of trouble.'*

Father Peter was not happy. But I thanked him for all he had done for my family, and I asked him to keep my suitcase, which contained all our important family documents. To this he willingly agreed. And on the morning we left he accompanied us on his bicycle, going on ahead and waiting for us, until we reached a place he thought was safe. May the Good Lord bless this His servant for fulfilling God's love for us.

I had a very small amount of money with me from the sale of a bull. On the road I met the man who had bought the bull; and with a word of sympathy he offered to buy another bull from me, at the full price and in the new currency. Gratefully I wrote out a letter of agreement, witnessed by a passer-by; and I went on, much richer now.

I should have been happy, but instead, for the first time, I was afraid, thinking I would be robbed. And then, just as it was getting dark, we crossed a main road, and heard military voices. Terrified, we ran into the long grass on the other side and dropped to the ground. My three children, who had bravely kept up with the adults' pace, huddled with me on some cut grass. Our hearts beat so loudly we thought they must be heard. The grass under my daughter Sarah moved – a big snake was sheltering there. And I put my hand in some human excrement, and could not rub it off properly.

But the soldiers did not find us, and that night we came to a home where a kind woman let us stay, and gave us water to wash, and even offered us supper.

The next day I sought temporary refuge with Mr Jackson, the Church Captain of the St August Church of Uganda, who had helped me at the beginning of my first exile in Kenya. But his relationship with my husband had made him a suspect of the new government, and both he and his wife were afraid to let us into their house. I told them of my plan to go to Lira, and said I needed their help not to stay, but only to find transport. This they immediately gave, though it was dangerous as well, since the eyes of the military were already on the Captain's movements.

The Captain found other friends to help, who established that only one lorry was going to Lira, and there were military all around. Disguising myself as best I could, I hurried with them and the children to the Lira road. Captain Jackson followed at a distance, so that he would not look part of our group.

On the way one of our friends, Joseph, said that if my name were on any of our belongings it should be removed. The only thing with my name on it was my Holy Bible; and to my horror and amazement Joseph took it, and tore out the page that bore my name. This violation hurt me as much as anything that had happened so far, and I could not hold back my tears.

Now the lorry was approaching. Joseph instructed the children to seal their mouths and not speak a word. We climbed on, and immediately I saw a few people I knew, one of them a dear friend of the family. How terrible it felt not to be able to exchange a single word, for fear of being revealed to the soldiers on board! All our freedom, all our human peace and comfort had been taken away from us: I felt that as never before on that lorry. All I could do was pray: 'Please God, see us through this journey, in the name of Your Son, Jesus Christ, our Lord.'

At the last road block a soldier announced that the lorry had broken down, and we should wait for help on board. But then there was another announcement: the families of soldiers should move to a Land Rover, which would take them to the bus station in Lira. I was afraid, and hesitated; but when I saw the woman I knew get out and join the soldiers' wives, I signalled to the children, and we all jumped out and onto the Land Rover as well.

It was nearly sunset when we arrived at Lira. My parents lived eight miles away, and there was no transport, so we had to spend the night in town. Most travellers slept on the veranda of the station hotel, but since it belonged to my cousin I asked for accommodation. My cousin was away, and we were very nearly refused; but in the last minute my cousin's children pleaded that we be let in. Thank God for that, because in the middle of the night we heard gunfire, which lasted until morning. We lay awake, each child holding on to the other, and my hand stretched as far as it could, to hold them all. In the morning we heard that some of the travellers on the veranda had been robbed, and in the gunfire we had heard several lives had been lost.

FILDA OTUNNU

A Story

Winter was arriving, an unnatural winter such that no one had ever remembered and no one had ever seen. Mountains, deserts, streets, cities, villages – all were utterly frozen. In place of snow, hailstones fell. They were so large they broke the stalks of flowers and the branches of trees. Everywhere was quiet, as though the people had died. The city had become a ghost city. No one had the courage to leave their homes.

Then snow and hail fell together in a great deluge. The deluge was so strong and cruel that it broke most of the trees on the land and most of the windows and doors of the houses. People in the cities and animals in the fields cowered in their burrows and waited for death.

There was no sign of deer, of rabbits or birds. All you could see were the wolves in the deserts, in the cities, in the villages. They searched everywhere with their blood-red eyes and open jaws, and with their claws ready to kill and tear. Wolfishly they prowled until they found a creature to rend and eat.

Silence reigned. There was no sound of birds singing, or rabbits scurrying, not even the baleful sound of vultures in the trees. The branches were snapped and broken, and all that remained were the trunks to perch on.

The fearful sounds and messages were brought, the messages of ruin, of cruelty and death

The people were so afraid, it was hard to be patient as they counted the seconds of the long long days. From their burrows they looked out at the sky and waited for the cloud that covered it to be cleansed: a cloud so thick and dark it made day and night the same.

They had only the messages of cold, of deluge and death

The people were plunged in despair, because we could not account

51

for the cloud which had brought the cold and the dark, perhaps forever. Where had it come from? From a cold climate it had come into our sky and our land, where everyone lived together. Out of that thick dark could came fear and hate and despair.

From our sky there came a maddening sound which smashed our ears and shook our homes. Whatever that sound touched changed to ashes. Wherever there were flowers, grass, people, birds or any living thing they were changed to fire and ashes.

Despair ruin and death

My life too was being changed, like all the others. When the deluge broke my window, I covered it with a sheet of iron, but I left a gap so that I could see when the dark cloud and the thick snow were over. I kept my eye fixed on god's sky and waited for the sun's chariot to return. But when would it come?

The deluge battered and shook the house, it broke my neighbour's windows and doors. I heard the sound and shared their fear. I heard the screams and weeping of women, of children, of men, and shared everything.

It was like the day that God had sent his flood upon Noah and all his tribe. Our future would be the future of Noah's tribe, when God wanted to give his help, but the people could not accept it.

Every time I tried to go out to help my neighbours and their children the cold and the rain and the snow stopped me. But what stopped me even more were the black wolves, looking for anything alive.

As I looked through my neighbours' broken windows and doors I saw a bird, shaking with cold. Its nest had been destroyed by the deluge, its mother had died, and it was trying to hide. I picked it up. Its feet and wings and beak were trembling. Should I take it to my neighbours' house or mine, or to some other warm place?

Just as I was thinking that I was holding it so gently it was growing quiet, a gust of ripped it from my hand. I tried to see where the storm had tossed it, but the rain lashed my eyes and I could not see. I could not find the bird, I could do nothing to help it, I was certain it would die. I began to cry, but my tears froze; I called out, but no one heard me. I screamed to God, as loud as I could, but I knew that I had not been heard, because the noise of the cloud was louder. It was so loud it drowned out every other voice.

I was in despair for the loss of the bird. After a long time I took hold of myself. I tried to walk – but I could not move. While I wept for the bird my feet had frozen and stuck to the ground. Confusion descended on me, I may have lost consciousness in the cold and the snow.

Suddenly I felt I was in another place. Everything was different – the sky, the land, the people. What has happened? Oh, my God –

Here the sky changed every minute, from rain to sun, from hot to cold. The people kept changing too, they were hard to understand. One day someone was your friend, but tomorrow was different….. Oh my God, where am I? What has happened?

The people don't look at each other, they don't speak to each other, they don't smile. They don't trust each other, they are like pieces of wood. I couldn't believe what I saw. I fell down, but nobody asked me who I was. After a while a police car came and took me away. They took me to a place I didn't recognise. Perhaps it was a hospital.

Someone came and asked me, 'Where are you from?' 'I am from Afghanistan,' I replied. As soon as the word 'Afghanistan' came out of my mouth they all disappeared. I was amazed. Did the ground swallow them up? Did they fly up into God's sky?

After a few minutes some other people appeared. I understood: they were afraid of me. Their faces were covered with masks, their bodies with long overalls.

'Are you from Afghanistan?' they asked.

'Yes,' I said. They looked at each other in surprise.

'What are you doing here?' they asked.

'I don't know,' I answered.

They laughed, all together. 'Why don't you know?'

So I told them my story, from beginning to end. When I had finished they conferred quietly. 'It's possible' – 'No, it's not' – 'Maybe the storm brought him' – 'Maybe he's just lying'…..

'How do you feel?' they asked.

I told them I felt as though my breath had stopped.

Again they looked surprised. One said: 'He must be telling the truth. He must come from a different planet, from a completely different climate.' They took me off to a laboratory to analyse. They have decided I am a different kind of being.

'Your body will have to be changed,' they told me.

'Why?' I asked.

'It's the only way to survive here,' they said. 'That way at least you may live for a short time. Otherwise you will die.'

I struggled to understand. Have I survived one disaster only to land in another? But then they told me that I would have to pay for my operation, and the price was very high. 'I haven't got any money,' I told them. Then they hadn't any choice. They decided I wasn't dangerous, and they let me go.

Now I am free, but I still have trouble breathing.

I have found some food that looks like the food at home, but it doesn't taste like the food at home. I cannot find a friend: every time I trust someone like a sister or brother, they change.

I must change or die
I am caught between death and change
I remember my life in my country, my land, my friends, my family
Every minute I feel I am dying. Only the blood and the breath I have brought from my country keeps me alive.

HASSAN BAMYANI

Here

… at the Orthodox
church in Paris, the last White
grey-haired Russians pray to God, who
is centuries younger than they and equally
helpless. In alien cities we'll
remain, like trees, like stones.

ADAM ZAGAJEWSKI, '*Song of an Émigré*'

'Florence Park': photograph by Daphne

Arrival

Never again to breathe pure happiness
My gorgeous memories withered like flowers
I smiled to tame my pain
So that my future could arrive
I laughed at myself, to help myself,
And sometimes I didn't know why

All my happiness is unreturning
Everything is unbeautiful
I think over and over, like an old song:
All is gone
I have nothing
All I have is missing
I miss everything,
Even myself

In a group I am alone
The wind swings me
From side to side
Ceaselessly
Even when the day is bright
For me it's night
I can't see my way
Why – how – where can I run?
How can I recover from my sickness?
Only God knows.

A new life is waiting
But I cannot take it
Yesterday will not let me go.
I must let it go.
My dreams must be
Not of yesterday but of today,

Or even better, tomorrow.
Decide nothing now.
Only tomorrow,
When each step will make
All my steps grow.

EDEN HABTEMICHAEL

Secretary

It's a job like any other:
Be nice to clients,
Polite to customers,
Answer their questions,
Give them advice

Smile and speak sweetly,
Treat everyone fairly.
This is the job description
Of a secretary.

But it didn't apply to Mary.
When I arrived in her office
I asked to speak to my solicitor
But she made me wait with the others
For a long time.

After a while she started to paint her nails.
'Have we met before?' she began.
'I don't think so,' I replied, but
She was not satisfied.
'Are you sure?'
'Yes. I have never been here before.'

Then she started to talk without stopping
About everyone's personal story.
'Her case is this', 'His case is that' –
She told everyone's secrets.

'Look at *him*, he's crazy.
And that one doesn't work, he's lazy.
And *that* one's a thief, a Mafia robber'
– she scattered her words loudly

One of the clients said, 'Excuse me,
Do you know him?'
'Yes,' she said, 'as well as my own family.
I don't remember his name,
But he's a murderer.'

'You don't know him,' the client said,
'He is my brother.'
'You're right,' she said, not at all bothered,
And immediately started again.

When I remember Mary
I think she was whatever she liked
Policeman and lawyer,
Judge and jury

With all those poor people
I think Mary was not just
A secretary

EDEN HABTEMICHAEL

Lovely Time

When I was first in England
I didn't like anything and was sad
   I cried all the time
   I dreamed only of home
   I missed my sweet husband, my mother

Then suddenly I got Indefinite Leave
My life changed immediately
   I came from London to Oxford
   And began to gather knowledge in my mind

Still it was a struggle
Life stayed hard and miserable

   Until one day I found a class
   Wow – I could go to an EMBS!

'I am your teacher, Jenny is my name,'
Said that kind and lovely woman.

   In the first meeting I was afraid
   My English was not good
   After that I grew confident
   In the lively class with funny students

Back home a mouse is an ugly intruder
But now, the key to my computer
   Keyboard, screen, printer, hardware
   Windows, I-con, menu, software
Verb, adjective, noun, sentence –
We did many exercises

Fabio laughed
Safedin was tired
Golshan always asked questions
Daz coughed
At lunch-time came Mehmoud
Our teacher smiled
Shamraz needed a break

Switch on, enter floppy
Log off, screen empty
    What's the matter
    With my computer?
    Ask our teacher
She helped everybody
We understood and were happy

    Day by day our class was smaller,
    The students were fewer,
Only three or four sometimes,
Sometimes only Eden at the computers

    That lovely moment will never come back again
    I so much miss everyone

Thank you for everything, our teacher.
I will never forget the 10th of September,
When I first saw the EMBS Centre,
When my hopes for the future began.

EDEN HABTEMICHAEL

Always in my Mind

Somebody
Is running in the dark
Climbing up a hill
Sliding down again

Where to go?
What to do?
Asked for help
The answer was no

It's so hard to explain
When you are disqualified
From the right lane
Your mind blocks

When you are new in this country
Will anyone give you rest and peace
To light your way
To a bright future?

Yes. I was right to come, really.
People are helpful and friendly.
They help you to fight
To break down the block

They help you to study,
Give you good advice, show you the true way.
There is a family atmosphere, *salaam,*
At Asylum Welcome

And now, amazing – we learn creative writing!
How to write short stories,
Use our own rhythms,
Express our ideas in poems, in diaries

I don't have words
To express the smallest part of how I feel.
How can I fill the sea
With my small spoon?

This is the product of your teaching, Carole,
Thank you too, and Asylum Welcome.
It is more blessed to give than to receive,
You are in my mind always.

EDEN HABTEMICHAEL

Sweet Lily

Sweet Lily for my eyes
Peace for my mind.

    I always knew that lovely voice
    Even while she was inside me.

I tried to speak to her
But she couldn't hear
I smiled at her
But she couldn't see
Perhaps they thought I was crazy

    When I heard music
    She danced
    When I was angry
    She stayed still
    As long as she was inside me
    I was warm.

It had to stop.
I opened my eyes on the white bed
The sweet feeling had changed
I heard unknown sounds
Those sounds – that pain – filled the night
I will never forget.

    A deep breath – she was born
    She is a diamond
    She is everything
    When I'm with her
    The sun is clean, the sky is bright
    I need no food, no drink, no money.

Sweet Lily, my daughter
When I'm with her
Life sings a great song.

EDEN HABTEMICHAEL

My Second home

Always I wake early
then I wash my teeth and my faice
I will try to help my mum
By changing my uniform
Checoflex is my favourite
With cold milk for breakfast
I am excited to get to school
I love my friends I like my teachear
their really kind

story time, writing, reading
With messy shirt painting, drawing
It is fun

our school is lovely
singing talking assembly
We learn loving eachother
ho hiting pushing remember?
to help my class
I am "school councillor

As I love my house
I love my schol St James
As I love my house.

— o —

Segen

SEGEN HABTEMICHAEL

'Travelator': photograph by Daphne

What is it Like to Live Here?

Everything seems to be all right.
There is no killer, no running for cover,
No keeping our bags packed
Every moment of the night and day.
But my heart does not rest.

We are safe now,
The children go to school,
We have a doctor, we even have a dentist,
Our bellies are full, our bodies are covered.
But my heart does not rest.

I have got all the training I need,
Plenty of jobs are advertised.
There is help available,
I feel eager to move on.
But my heart does not rest.

So many times, back there,
We tilled, and sowed, and weeded.
Then, just as we were about to reap,
Our harvest was taken away.
And now my heart does not rest.

Is it my imagination,
Or is it happening here?
Every time I train, and learn, and apply,
Is my harvest snatched away?
Let me trust, Lord, and at last my heart will rest.

FILDA OTUNNU

Life Changes

When I was growing up I had a friend called Kori. As kids, he and I and other friends used to play games like football, throwing stones and swimming. From time to time we all liked going to the wood, climbing trees and picking fruit. We would come home at sunset exhausted but happy, our clothes dirty and torn.

The years passed by and we reached adulthood.

We started organising football teams, going out to meet in cafés, chatting and catching up on news. Some of us got married and others had girlfriends. We were no longer single, and had many responsibilities to shoulder. The married ones all lost touch a bit, because they were spending most of their time with their families; others were working the land, or running their own businesses. Some travelled abroad, like myself.

When I came to England I left behind my best friend Kori and my family and found a new life. I tried very hard to work out how to fit in, to achieve something worthwhile and make up for what I had lost. Many times I felt like an alien, not only to the people of this country, but to my best and closest friend Kori as well.

When I made phone calls to Kori he kept saying: 'Do not forget your people and your country; keep company with your own people.' And I thought: 'My friend cannot understand.' Soon I grew bored, and realised there was no closeness or warmth between us any more.

MOHAMMED ISSA

'Kenyan girl': photograph by Rory Carnegie

The Children

In the boundless afternoon
the children are walking
with their gentle grammar on their lips

From door to door
the little ones go, brightly tranquil,
repenting nothing

How safe their journey,
how placid their voyage,
famous and simple

Whisper to me as though I were a child,
and let my answer
be your oracle and mine.

Panic may still trouble us,
the archaeology of our past,
but we are pursuing that adult dark
with the lamps of innocence

Soon our message will reach you, our gospel.
Free at last, happy at last,
we have gone away
into the wise world of the children.

WAKUNYEKI MUKOBYA

My Flowers

Among flowers
I prefer meridiens,
continuous circles that cry
and come ashore amid blood

Preferring flowers,
wild or cultivated,
I wipe up weather
and careworn clouds

Preferring flowers,
it's hard for me to fathom
the waves, their soft cunning,
the shores they mark and erode

Preferring flowers,
the sky unsettles me

I prefer flowers
To the earth's monotony,
a life lived within earshot of leaves

But far out at sea
the future of flowers is planned,
the story of flowering
is rooted in the horizon.

WAKUNYEKI MUKOBYA

The Women

Women waiting for their husbands
Sit among dahlias all afternoon,
While quiet processional seasons
Drift and subside at their door like dunes,
And echoes of the ocean curl from their flowered walls.

The room is a murmuring shell of nothing at all.
As the fire dies under the dahlias, shifting embers
Flake from the silence, thundering when they fall.
Faithful wives waken, still bathed in slumber,
The loud tide breaks and turns to bring them breath.

At five o'clock it flows around their deaths,
And then the dahlias, whirling.
Suddenly catherine wheels of surf
Spin on their stems until the shallows sing,
And flower pools gleam like lamps on the lifeless tables.

WAKUNYEKI MUKOBYA

Operation

You are carried in a basket,
   Like a carcass from the shambles,
   To the theatre, a cockpit,
   Where they stretch you on a table.

They bid you close your eyelids,
   And they mask you with a napkin,
   And the anaesthetic reaches
   Hot and subtle through your being

And you gasp and reel and shudder
   In a rushing, swaying rapture,
   While the voice at your elbow
   Fades – receding – fainter – farther

Then the lights grow fast and furious
   And you hear a noise of waters
   And you wrestle, blind and dizzy,
   In an agony of effort

Till a sudden lull accepts you
   And you sound an utter darkness …
   And awaken, with a struggle,
   To a hushed and waiting room

WAKUNYEKI MUKOBYA

Living in England

Living in England,
Oxford says, is the price you pay
For not living in New England

Living in the UK,
Oxford thinks, is a reward
For managing not to live anywhere else

The rest of the country?
Sagging between two poles
Of tasteless decoration and worse weather

No. Look closely.
Under cover of light and sound
Both shores are hurrying towards each other

Cardiff is already halfway to London,
Birmingham is nervously losing its way
To Detroit

Desperately, the inhabitants
Hope to be saved in the middle,
Pray to the mountains and sea

To keep them apart.

WAKUNYEKI MUKOBYA

Sous-Entendu

Don't think

that I don't know
that as you talk
the hand of your mind
is secretly
undressing me

Don't think

that I don't know
that you know
that everything I reply
is clothing

WAKUNYEKI MUKOBYA

'Somali girl': photograph by Cecilia

School

Her slippers have no toe or heel.
Her own torn feet transport
Her body to school

But the last thin strips of felt and sole
Around her tender instep
Transport her mind

HASSAN BAMYANI

A Lie Fire

A lie fire
a hate fire
is this world

There is
no love
no laughter
no smile
no help

There is no thought
but how to cheat
how to sell oneself
how to suck another dry

In this lie fire
my left hand
doesn't understand my right

Every part of my body
is the enemy of every other
in the hate fire
of this world

HASSAN BAMYANI

The Rug Speaks

I am made of the blood
   of children's fingers

I am made of their suffering,
day and night,
the suffering of their eyes,
their backs,
   their bodies

Why do you give me
only your feet,
your shoes,
   the soles of your shoes?

You don't understand me,
you don't know where I come from,
   who I am.

HASSAN BAMYANI

Untitled

My body is on fire
I leap into the cold water
but I am still burning
the fire has moved from outside me

in

If I leap into the dark water
I drown
if I don't leap
I burn

There is fire
here is water
this water would drown
the best swimmer in the world

The fire burned me
to a handful of ashes
but the deep water
swallows me up,

leaving
not even ashes, not even smoke

Which is better, fire or water?
I prefer fire
it is more generous
it leaves me my smoke and ashes

I send out a scream
As far as I can:

Come, fire,
I love you
More than the cold dark deep

HASSAN BAMYANI

Two Poems

I.

In my bowl
You've poured perfume

How can you favour me, give me your gift?
How can you want me still?

I am so far from the sun
And you are the sun of suns

You will be covered with cloud
Until I am clean

Until I can show myself to you
And you to me once more.

II.

My feet and head were covered in mud,
In disappointment and fear, in not knowing and shame

My feet moved
I stood up

The water washed me
No mud or dirt now

My body is clean
I don't feel shame any more

HASSAN BAMYANI

I See I am Dying

I was a high mountain
Higher than everything
Full of power
Full of pride

I looked down at everything
I didn't know weakness
I didn't know exhaustion
I didn't know fear

My weight was as a mountain
My going was as a river that came down from a mountain
My laughing was as a wave
I gave help to everyone

I didn't know
That one day I would be dying
Diminishing
But now I see

The heavy rain over my peak
Is eroding me day by day
I am becoming a plain
A desert

Everyone walks on me
Nobody feels my pain
I see
I am dying

HASSAN BAMYANI

Song of the Sun

Sun, I am your son.
No – I am your lover,
I am your servant.
You adorn me,
You are my spring water.

But you are so far
away.

Please don't leave me,
please talk to me,
let me kiss you,
let me hug you close
again

Without you
I am so cold,
so dark,
so thirsty,

Without you, so
alone

so
afraid

HASSAN BAMANYI

My Body

Most of my body is burning.
Suffering, starving,
Dying of thirst,
My legs unable to walk,
My blood unable to flow

And yet a part of me
Is happy, dancing
in a garden,
not knowing what is happening
to the rest

Is this natural?
Is it right?
No!
This is shame,
This is betrayal.
All must dance,
Or none.

HASSAN BAMANYI

Cruel Fire

I am used to burning
You cannot frighten me
I burn and burn until my smoke
Extinguishes your fire

My smoke is stronger
Than your fire
I am not iron
I am steel, friend of fire

You cannot melt me
I stand until
You are extinguished
and exhausted,
Cruel fire.

HASSAN BAMANYI

I Have Seen Stars in your Hair and Fountains in your Eyes

I have seen stars in your hair and fountains in your eyes
Your face speaks to me of the sun
It makes my body bake and my heart beat
   When I tell my story of love
   Your lips listen with love

Your kiss would awake me
Or else burn me
I am afraid
I am a moth around the candle of your lips
A fish in the ocean of your eyes
   Don't turn your eyes away
   Listen to my story of love

You are my world, my time, my joy
Life without love is a body without a soul
Call me and I'll kiss your hair
You are spring flowers, spring air
Without you I am autumn
You are my sun
Look down on my winter body
   Warm me
   Restore my life

HASSAN BAMANYI

I Love

I love flowers because of their perfume

I love buds because they stand for my love's lips

I love spring because it stands for renewal

I love the moon because its face is like my love's face

I love the sun because its heat is like my love's embrace

I love the waves because they are like my love's hair

I love the ibex because she stole my love's eyes

I love the river because it is as clear as my love's heart

I love love because it burns me

I love the burning because it keeps me alive

I love my life because it gave me my love

HASSAN BAMANYI

Epilogue

Two poems by Carole Angier, the first inspired by a story of Filda's, the second by something Hassan said, quoted in the opening lines

'Asylum Welcome': photograph by Graham Wilkins

Fifty Years

Fifty years after the Russian farm-boys
rode in under *Arbeit Macht Frei*
and freed her,
she went for a stroll without her sweater
for the first time.

And today, 2004,
a young man, not yet thirty,
still, five years after
Uganda, cannot walk out the door
without his suitcase in his hand.

How can I tell him he
has forty-five years to go?
In my dreams women carrying their sweaters,
men carrying their suitcases,
ceaselessly wander the world.

CAROLE ANGIER

Technology

'Technology
doesn't feel you,' he said.
'Machines don't hear you like a man.'
Somehow he'd kept this faith,
even though the machine-men
cut him down

When
that old doubter, Descartes,
announced he'd located the soul
in a gland, philosophers
mocked. Still,
we want it to be somewhere

So
it's in the amygdala now.
That's where
the chip of fellow-feeling hides,
that's where
I hear your cries

But
we also know this:
that it can be switched off
by some old tale of woe,
or
never switched on at all

Then
the eye does not light, nor the hand
flinch from the blow.

Then the machines don't hear,
then the technology
doesn't feel

CAROLE ANGIER